PRINCIPLES OF IGNATIAN LEADERSHIP

A Resource for a Faith-Committed Life

WILLIAM J. BYRON, SJ, and
JAMES L. CONNOR, SJ

Paulist Press
New York / Mahwah, NJ

Cover images: IHS symbol by Eziutka, courtesy of Thinkstock. Light blue, textured-background image by tawanlubfah/Shutterstock.com.
Cover and book design by Lynn Else

Library of Congress Cataloging-in-Publication Data

Byron, William J., 1927–
    Principles of Ignatian leadership : a resource for a faith-committed life / William J. Byron, S.J. and James L. Connor, S.J.
        pages cm
    Includes bibliographical references.
    ISBN 978-0-8091-4965-0 (pbk. : alk. paper) — ISBN 978-1-58768-577-4 (ebook)
    1. Ignatius, of Loyola, Saint, 1491–1556. 2. Spiritual life—Catholic Church. 3. Spirituality—Catholic Church. 4. Leadership—Religious aspects—Catholic Church. I. Title.
    BX4700.L7B97 2016
    248.4`82—dc23

                                                                            2015016556

ISBN 978-0-8091-4965-0 (paperback)
ISBN 978-1-58768-577-4 (e-book)

Published by Paulist Press
997 Macarthur Boulevard
Mahwah, New Jersey 07430

www.paulistpress.com

Printed and bound in the
United States of America

PRINCIPLES OF IGNATIAN LEADERSHIP

In memory of Pedro Arrupe,
Jesuit General (1965–1983)
A Great Leader

Contents

Introduction

This resource book for leaders identifies and explains Ignatian principles of leadership. They are Ignatian principles of leadership because they are rooted in the person, writings, and life of St. Ignatius of Loyola (1491–1556), founder of the Society of Jesus—the Jesuit Order.

This book will be of particular interest because it helps to interpret the mind and heart of our first Jesuit pope. The spirituality of Pope Francis is Ignatian. His choice of the name Francis pays special respect to St. Francis of Assisi, the "Poverello," and suggests that Franciscan spirituality may guide his leadership style, particularly his concern for the poor. However, the spirituality that has shaped his character and influenced his choices is Ignatian. Hence, in order to understand why and how Pope Francis leads as he does, one has to understand the principles of Ignatian leadership.

In calling these principles *Ignatian*—not simply Jesuit—we emphasize their broader applicability, beyond Jesuit organizational life, to leadership in any organization, including leadership in completely secular settings far removed from church and religious life.

Our purpose is to encourage those who are responsible for alumni associations of Jesuit schools, colleges, and universities, to invite their graduates—men and women with leadership potential—to form local groups for leadership training, small groups for once-a-month prayer, reflection, and discussion, that will enable them to internalize these Ignatian principles and then apply them wherever they happen to be in the world of work and organizational life. While the origin of these principles is spiritual, for the most part, their application will take place in secular settings. Based on Ignatian and Jesuit spirituality, they will be of particular relevance to graduates of Jesuit schools whose education was rooted in these same faith-based principles. But as the success and almost universal appeal of Pope Francis demonstrates, these principles are both timely and needed worldwide today.

To begin, we offer, therefore, a summary of the life of Ignatius and the Order he founded.

IGNATIUS OF LOYOLA AND THE ORIGINS OF THE SOCIETY OF JESUS

Iñigo Lopez de Loyola was born in the Basque country of Spain in 1491. Loyola was the name of his ancestors' family house and farmland in northern Spain. Iñigo was his given name; it was later changed to Ignatius. He and his brothers were in various capacities in service to the kings of Castile.

He was seriously wounded by the French at Pamplona in May of 1521 when a cannonball shattered his right leg and wounded his left. During a long recuperation, the future saint had what he describes as his first reasoning, his first reflective experience of the things of God.

In his third-person autobiography, Ignatius writes, "Up to his twenty-sixth year he was a man given over to the vanities of the world, and took a special delight in the exercise of arms, with a great and vain desire of winning glory." While recuperating, he read from the only two books available to him—a life of Christ and stories about the saints. He also daydreamed of performing exploits of chivalry that attracted the attention of a beautiful noblewoman. He noticed that his reading and his daydreams left him with different feelings. He experienced enthusiasm (*consolation*) after reading about Christ and the saints, but he felt disconsolate and empty (*desolation*) in the wake of his daydreams. From this reflective experience, he subsequently developed the practice of what is called "discernment of spirits."

Upon recovery, he made his way in 1522 to the Benedictine Monastery at Montserrat in Spain, sought out a confessor, and unburdened his soul in a general confession. Then, during a "Knight's Vigil," he hung up his sword and dagger—emblems of a swashbuckling past—at the famous Shrine of the Black Madonna (a statue blackened over time by carbon from the candles constantly burning beneath it).

Ignatius spent the next eleven months in prayer in the nearby village of Manresa, where he experienced interior trials as well as divine illuminations. At Manresa, he underwent a spiritual transformation, an experience he would later draw upon in producing his *Spiritual Exercises*, a handbook intended to serve as an outline for a month-long period of prayer and reflection. Near Manresa, on the banks of the River Cardoner, Ignatius received an illumination that gave him an awareness of the loving presence of God in all things.

After Manresa, he began referring to himself as "the pilgrim." In 1523, Ignatius made a pilgrimage to Jerusalem to visit the places made holy by the presence of Christ—the Holy Sepulcher, the river Jordan, Bethlehem, and the Mount of Olives.

At age 33, he began to study grammar with children in Barcelona, so that he could move on to higher studies subsequently in Paris. As one historian wrote, "He applied his untrained mind for two laborious years to the mastery of Latin declensions and conjugations."[*]

While pursuing university studies in Alcalá in 1526, he was twice imprisoned by the Inquisition over issues

---

[*]William V. Bangert, *A History of the Society of Jesus* (Chestnut Hill, MA: Institute of Jesuit Sources, 1985), 12.

of clothing and preaching, and jailed again in 1527 in Salamanca when the orthodoxy of his book of spiritual exercises and his spiritual teaching were questioned. He was cleared but decided to leave Spain and head for Paris to further his studies.

Beginning in 1528, Ignatius spent seven years in Paris studying grammar, philosophy, and theology. It was there, especially at the University of Paris, where, after lengthy preparation, he began giving the Spiritual Exercises to his first companions. Gradually, the small band of brothers formed what was to become the Society of Jesus.

On August 15, 1534, Ignatius and six of his early followers (Peter Faber, Francis Xavier, Simón Rodríguez, Diego Laínez, Alonso Salmerón, and Nicolás Bobadilla) walked from the Latin Quarter of Paris to the chapel of St. Denis on the slope of Montmartre, where Faber, the only priest among them, celebrated Mass, and all seven pronounced the vows of poverty, chastity, and a commitment to go on pilgrimage to the Holy Land, failing that, to offer themselves in service to the pope. Three others from the University of Paris—Claude Le Jay, Paschase Broët, and Jean Codure—subsequently joined the group that began to identify itself as the "Company of Jesus."

Ignatius was ordained a priest in Venice on June 24, 1537.

In a wayside chapel in the village of La Storta in November 1537, while enroute to Rome, Ignatius, accompanied by Faber and Lainez, experienced a vision of God the Father looking upon Christ his Son carrying the Cross. Both looked on Ignatius with love, and Ignatius heard the Son say to him, "I want you [Ignatius] to serve us [Christ and the Father]." And he also heard the Father say, "I shall be propitious to you [plural, therefore referring to Ignatius and his companions] in Rome."

In Rome, on September 27, 1540, Pope Paul III gave formal approval to the establishment of the Society of Jesus as a fully canonical religious order.

❧

The Jesuit Order, founded on Ignatian principles, has numbered in its own ranks outstanding leaders. However, importantly, through their educational ministries, the Jesuits have produced notable lay leaders who have something special to offer the world.

Ignatian principles are countercultural; they are grounded in the gospel of Jesus Christ and stand in opposition to the dominant values of secular culture. Ignatius would identify those dominant secular values as "riches...honor...pride" (*Spiritual Exercises* 142). The countercultural values he recommends are "poverty... insults...humility" (*Spiritual Exercises* 146). These will be explained in subsequent sections of this book.

The challenge of this book is to translate authentic Ignatian principles into practical guidelines for effective leadership in contemporary secular culture.

We aim to open a door and welcome you to step inside. Furthermore, we remind those who have been touched in any way by Ignatian influences earlier in their lives that Ignatius referred to himself in his early post-conversion years as a "pilgrim." May his pilgrimage and yours converge on the path to leadership in a world that needs you more than we can express.

WJB and JLC

1

First Principle and Foundation

You are created to praise, reverence, and serve God your Lord, and by this means to save your soul.

The other things on the face of the earth are created for you to help you in attaining the end for which you are created.

Hence, you are to make use of them in so far as they help you in the attainment of your end, and you must rid yourself of them in so far as they prove a hindrance to you.

Therefore, you should make yourself indifferent to all created things, as far as you are allowed free choice and are not under any prohibition. Consequently, as far as you are concerned, you should not prefer health to sickness, riches to poverty, honor to dishonor, a long life to a short life. The same holds for all other things.

Your one desire and choice should be what is more conducive to the end for which you are created.

~ Ignatius of Loyola, *Spiritual Exercises* 23

These several short paragraphs at the beginning of his book, *Spiritual Exercises,* constitute what Ignatius of Loyola calls the "First Principle and Foundation" (no. 23). These words can serve as a personal mission statement for those who see life and faith from an Ignatian and Jesuit perspective. They emphasize God's intent that all humans pursue a single ultimate end in life, namely, loving service. They further stress that all other created things are meant to be a means toward this ultimate goal.

Leadership Lesson

If you keep in mind an awareness of your ultimate purpose, you will choose wisely and lead well. If you are properly "indifferent," that is, free of disordered attachments to created things, your freedom and sense of purpose will provide clear direction for your leadership.

REFLECTION

Why "principle"? Why "foundation"?
Can these few paragraphs become an organizing
principle around which you can build your life?

2

Generosity

Dear Lord,
teach me to be generous
teach me to serve you as you deserve to be served
to give and not to count the cost;
to fight and not to heed the wounds;
to toil and not to seek for rest;
to labor and not to ask for any reward,
save that of knowing that I am doing your will,
*   O God.*
                        ~ Prayer of St. Ignatius, source unknown

It takes spiritual maturity to catch the Ignatian vision, to see, for example, the "Principle and Foundation" as a basis for living—as a focus that helps one find God and God's love in all things. It takes additional spiritual maturity to be willing to make your own the famous Ignatian prayer for generosity that is presented above.

Leadership Lesson

Selfless service in accordance with the will of God is an essential characteristic of Ignatian leadership.

REFLECTION

Why is it that a generous person is
particularly qualified to become
an effective leader?

3

Ad Maiorem Dei Gloriam

The initials A.M.D.G., which mean "to God's greater glory," appear on the logo or "coat of arms" of many Jesuit institutions and organizations.

Ignatius of Loyola understood the "greater glory of God" to involve a greater, more generous, and selfless service to others. And, for Ignatius, the help of souls meant the help of bodies too, because he sent his men into hospitals for the care of the poor, into cities for the protection of prostitutes and marginated people, and into classrooms for the religious instruction of unsophisticated children.

Ignatius had a tendency to see life as a struggle between the forces of good and the forces of evil. He was a mystic who saw the world from God's viewpoint. He founded his religious order—the Jesuits—for like-minded men called, as he was, to be contemplatives in action. Ignatius and his first companions committed themselves *"to travel anywhere in the world where there is hope of God's greater glory and the good of souls."*

Leadership Lesson

The Jesuit motto, *Ad Maiorem Dei Gloriam,* suggests the following leadership lesson:

Ignatian leadership keeps looking higher—to the greater good of others and to the greater glory of God.

REFLECTION

In all areas of life, does your reach
exceed your grasp? If so, why is that
satisfying and not frustrating?

4

Magis

Those who wish to give greater proof of their love, and to distinguish themselves in the service of the eternal King and the Lord of all, will not only offer themselves entirely for the work, but will act against their sensuality and carnal and worldly love, and make offerings of greater value and of more importance in words such as these:

Eternal Lord of all things, in the presence of Thy infinite goodness, and of Thy glorious mother, and of all the saints of Thy heavenly court, this is the offering of myself which I make with Thy favor and help. I protest that it is my earnest desire and my deliberate choice, provided only it is for Thy greater service and praise, to imitate Thee in bearing all wrongs and all abuse and all poverty, both actual and spiritual, should Thy most holy majesty deign to choose and admit me to such a state and way of life.

~ Spiritual Exercises 97–98

A key meditation in the *Spiritual Exercises* is a prayerful engagement of the imagination that invites the one making the Exercises to consider "The Call of an Earthly

King" (no. 91) and to compare it with the call and reign of Christ the King (no. 95).

Note the words *greater* and *more* in the text; they are the foundation for the Jesuit theme of "the *magis*"—the fuller stretch, the higher reach, the extra effort. The *magis* resides in the human heart. It frames the Ignatian vision. It focuses any properly Ignatian initiative.

Leadership Lesson

The *"magis"* theme supports the following Ignatian leadership lesson:

Whatever the initiative, the objective is always to move toward the greater and the more.

REFLECTION

If indeed your reach does exceed your grasp,
can this be seen as evidence of the presence
of the *magis* in your life?

5

Incarnation

This will consist in calling to mind the history of the subject I have to contemplate. Here it will be how the Three Divine Persons look down upon the whole expanse or circuit of all the earth, filled with human beings. Since They see that all are going down to hell, They decree in Their eternity that the Second Person should become man to save the human race.

~ Spiritual Exercises 102

There is an Ignatian perspective here, quite literally, a point of view—it is from all eternity. The Ignatian outlook is comprehensive and universal—seeing "those on the face of the earth, in such great diversity in dress and in manner of acting. Some are white, some black; some at peace, and some at war; some weeping, some laughing; some well, some sick; some coming into the world, and some dying....I will see and consider the Three Divine Persons seated on the royal dais or throne of the Divine Majesty. They look down upon the whole surface of the earth, and behold all nations in great blindness, going down to death and descending into hell" (*Spiritual Exercises* 106). "I will also hear what the Divine Persons say, that is, 'Let us work the redemption of the human race'" (no. 107).

"I will think over what I ought to say to the Three Divine Persons, or to the eternal Word incarnate.... According to the light I have received, I will beg for grace to follow and imitate more closely our Lord, who has just become man for me" (no. 109).

The contemplation on the Incarnation provides a specifically Ignatian worldview. All things human belong in the Ignatian vision. The Ignatian eye sees the world in the light of eternity; sees all creation as good, and sees participation in the work of redemption as the Jesuit vocation.

Leadership Lesson

According to the Incarnational worldview of St. Ignatius:

Accept the fact of human solidarity and acknowledge the importance of excluding no place and no person from any effort to improve the human condition.

REFLECTION

See yourself and your world from a mile-high perspective, the way the triune God looks down upon the world. How does this influence your self-understanding?

6

Poverty, Insults, Humility

Consider how the Lord of all the world chooses so many persons, apostles, disciples, and the like. He sends them throughout the whole world, to spread his doctrine among people of every state and condition.

Consider the address which Christ our Lord makes to all his servants and friends whom he is sending on this expedition. He recommends that they endeavor to aid all persons, by attracting them, first, to the most perfect spiritual poverty and also, if the Divine Majesty should be served and should wish to choose them for it, even to no less a degree of actual poverty; and second, by attracting them to a desire for reproaches and contempt, since from these results humility.

In this way there will be three steps: the first, poverty in opposition to riches; the second, reproaches or contempt in opposition to honor from the world; and the third, humility in opposition to pride. Then from these three steps they should induce people to all the other virtues.

~ Spiritual Exercises 145–46

In the *Spiritual Exercises,* there is the "Meditation on Two Standards,"—"the one of Christ, our Supreme Commander and Lord, the other of Lucifer, the mortal enemy of our human nature" (no. 136). The above paragraphs pertain to the Standard of Christ (nos. 145–46). Ignatius states that "Christ calls and desires all persons to come under his standard" (no. 137) and then invites the retreatant, in an exercise of the imagination, to place him or herself in the presence of Christ and listen.

Leadership Lesson

The Standard of Christ offers this counter-cultural Ignatian principle of leadership:

The three steps to genuine success are poverty as opposed to riches; insults or contempt as opposed to the honor of this world; humility as opposed to pride. "From these three steps, let them lead men to all other virtues" (no. 146).

REFLECTION

It was remarked in 2008 by Jesuit Cardinal Carlos Martini that delivery of the *Spiritual Exercises,* particularly the proclamation of the Standard of Christ, is "the service that the Society of Jesus is called to perform for the Church today."

How are poverty, insults, and humility encountered today by ordinary people leading ordinary lives?

7

The Cross

*Whoever wishes to serve as a soldier of God
beneath the banner of the cross in our Society,
which we desire to be designated by the name of
Jesus, and to serve the Lord alone and his vicar on
earth, should keep in mind that once he has made
a solemn vow of perpetual chastity he is a member
of a community founded chiefly for this purpose: to
strive especially for the progress of souls in
Christian life and doctrine and for the propagation
of the faith by the ministry of the word, by spiritual
exercises and works of charity, and specifically by
the education of children and unlettered persons in
Christianity.*

~ *Formula* or Statutes of the Society of Jesus

There is a famous phrase, "beneath the banner of the cross," in the *Formula* of the Institute of the Society of Jesus, approved in 1540 by Pope Paul III, thus marking the formal establishment of the Society of Jesus. "Beneath the banner of the cross" has special meaning for all Jesuits and special relevance in the tradition of Ignatian spirituality.

Leadership Lesson

The leadership principle to be derived from this portion of the Ignatian and Jesuit heritage might best be communicated in these words of Mahatma Gandhi:

"There comes a time when an individual becomes irresistible and his action becomes all-pervasive in its effects. This is when he reduces himself to zero."[1]

REFLECTION

Do you welcome or withdraw from the banner of the cross in your working life?

8

The Examen

Steps in Making the Ignatian Examen

1. We begin by quieting ourselves. Become aware of God's goodness, the gifts of life and love. Be thankful. Recall that without faith, the eye of love, the human world seems too evil for God to be good, for a good God to exist.

2. Pray for the grace to see clearly, to understand accurately, and to respond generously to the guidance God is giving us in our daily history.

3. Review in memory the history of the day (week, month, etc.) in order to be shown concrete instances of the presence and guidance of God and, perhaps, of the activity and influence of evil. These can be detected by paying attention to strong feelings we experienced that may have accompanied or arisen from situations and encounters.

4. Evaluate these instances in which we have either collaborated with God or yielded to the influence of evil in some way. Express gratitude and regret.

5. Plan and decide how to collaborate more effectively with God and how, with God's

*assistance, to avoid or overcome the influence of
evil in the future.*

Conclude with an "Our Father."

~ Spiritual Exercises 43

The Examen is an essential and daily component of
Ignatian prayer. This exercise, which is recommended to
be made at midday and in the evening before retiring,
involves five steps:

1. Thanksgiving;
2. Request for enlightenment;
3. Review of failings (as well as moments of
   grace);
4. Request for pardon; and
5. Resolve to mend my ways.

Leadership Lesson

The leadership lesson to be derived from
the practice of the Examen is that Gratitude
keeps the leader grounded in God's presence;
the daily Examen, opening with an expression
of gratitude, cultivates awareness of one's call
to faithful service.

REFLECTION

Do you agree with Socrates that
"the unexamined life is not worth living"?

9

Presupposition

It is necessary to suppose that every good Christian is more ready to put a good interpretation on another's statement than to condemn it as false. If an orthodox construction cannot be put on a proposition, the one who made it should be asked how he understands it. If he is in error, he should be corrected with all kindness. If this does not suffice, all appropriate means should be used to bring him to a correct interpretation, and so defend the proposition from error.

~ Spiritual Exercises 22

This famous "presupposition," stated early in the *Spiritual Exercises*, is a guiding principle for all effective leadership. It leads to a predisposition that shapes the character of a good leader.

Leadership Lesson

The leadership lesson to be learned from this "presupposition":

Think positively and listen receptively when others speak. Error on the part of another is not to be presumed, although once detected, error is to be corrected with kindness.

REFLECTION

This "presupposition" might be understood and adopted as a "predisposition"; if so, it can shape one's outlook on life, even becoming an organizing principle for one's interaction with others.
How might that work?

10

Discernment of Spirits

Ignatius offers *"rules for understanding to some extent the different movements produced in the soul and for recognizing those that are good, to admit them, and those that are bad, to reject them."*
~ *Spiritual Exercises* 313

In dealing with persons leading a seriously sinful life, the *evil* spirit will "fill their imagination with sensual delights and gratifications, the more readily to keep them in their vices and increase the number of their sins. With such persons the *good* spirit...will rouse the sting of conscience and fill them with remorse" (*Spiritual Exercises* 314).

"In the case of those who...seek to rise in the service of God to greater perfection...it is characteristic of the *evil* spirit to harass with anxiety, to afflict with sadness, to raise obstacles backed by fallacious reasonings that disturb the soul. Thus he [the evil spirit] seeks to prevent the soul from advancing. It is characteristic of the *good* spirit, however, to give courage and strength, consolations, tears, inspirations, and peace. This he [the good spirit] does by making all easy, by removing all obstacles so that the soul goes forward in doing good" (no. 315).

First, you have to locate yourself (are you on the slippery slope to sin or the upward path to virtue?); then you identify the source (good or evil spirit) of the feeling or mood you are experiencing. If you are on a downward moral slope, the feeling of delight is coming from the evil spirit; a feeling of remorse is from the good spirit. If you are on the moral upside, sadness and anxiety have their source in the evil spirit; a sense of peace is from the good spirit.

Note especially that good and evil spirits are at work in the world. The "push" or "pull" within you can be from God or not from God. You have to discern the origin of a particular "movement" or feeling, and in order to do that you have to give yourself a fair reading of where you stand before God. Are you moving away—on the downward slope; or trying to let yourself be drawn toward God—moving in the right direction? Beware of anxiety and discouragement when you are doing your best to move toward God; they are from the evil spirit! Heed the pangs of conscience when you are on the down side; the good spirit is trying to get through to you.

Leadership Lesson

The leadership lesson to be learned from an awareness of the "movements" of your soul:

Leaders decide; deciding is essential to leadership. But leaders first have to discern accurately in order to decide well. Hence they must first locate themselves (self-awareness) and be sufficiently "quiet" to detect the movements of competing spirits in a world where both good and evil spirits are at work.

REFLECTION

Can you locate the source of your anxieties?

11

Consolation

I call it consolation when an interior movement is aroused in the soul, by which it [the soul] is inflamed with love of its Creator and Lord, and as a consequence, can love no creature on the face of the earth for its own sake, but only in the Creator of them all. It is likewise consolation when one sheds tears that move [him or her] to the love of God, whether it be because of sorrow for sins, or because of the sufferings of Christ our Lord, or for any other reason that is immediately directed to the praise and service of God. Finally, I call consolation every increase of faith, hope, and love, and all interior joy that invites and attracts to what is heavenly and to the salvation of one's soul by filling it with peace and quiet in Christ our Lord.

~ Spiritual Exercises **316**

"Consolation" is a feeling, a movement within the soul. Ask yourself how you are feeling, and consolation, as described by Ignatius, may well describe your feeling. If that's the case, great! Presumably, the source of the consolation that Ignatius describes is God. "In consolation, the good spirit guides and counsels us" (*Spiritual Exercises* 318).

"God alone can give consolation to the soul without any previous cause…, that is, without any preceding perception or knowledge of any subject by which a soul might be led to such a consolation through its own acts of intellect and will" (no. 330). "If a cause precedes, then both the good angel and the evil spirit can give consolation to a soul, but for a quite different purpose. The good angel consoles for the progress of the soul, that it may advance and rise to what is more perfect. The evil spirit consoles for purposes that are the contrary, and that afterwards he [the evil spirit] might draw the soul to perverse intentions and wickedness" (no. 331). "It is a mark of the evil spirit to assume the appearance of an angel of light" (no. 332).

Leadership Lesson

A leadership lesson to be derived from the Ignatian description of "consolation":

An emotional environment of "peace and quiet," especially in the midst of great crisis and stress, is essential for effective leadership. Ignatius associates hope with consolation. Without hope in his or her heart, it is useless for a leader to try to lead.

REFLECTION

If your life is anchored in hope, you will experience an inner peace that only you can choose to let go.

12

Desolation

I call desolation what is entirely the opposite of what is described [above] as consolation. Desolation is darkness of soul, turmoil of spirit, inclination to what is low and earthly, restlessness rising from many disturbances and temptations which lead to want of faith, want of hope, want of love. The soul is wholly slothful, tepid, sad, and separated, as it were, from its Creator and Lord. For just as consolation is the opposite of desolation, so the thoughts that spring from consolation are the opposite of those that spring from desolation.

In time of desolation we should never make any change, but remain firm and constant in the resolution and decision which guided us the day before the desolation, or in the decision to which we adhered in the preceding consolation. For just as in consolation the good spirit guides and counsels us, so in desolation the evil spirit guides and counsels. Following his counsels we can never find the way to a right decision.

Though in desolation we must never change our former resolutions, it will be very advantageous to intensify our activity against the desolation. We can insist more upon prayer, upon meditation, and on much examination of ourselves. We can make an effort in a suitable way to do some penance.

When one is in desolation, he should be mindful that God has left him to his natural powers to resist the different agitations and temptations of the enemy in order to try him. He can resist with the help of God, which always remains, though he may not clearly perceive it....

When one is in desolation, he should strive to persevere in patience.

~ Spiritual Exercises 317–21

"The principal reasons why we suffer from desolation are three:"

1. "We have been tepid and slothful or negligent in our exercises of piety";
2. "God wishes to try us, to see how much we are worth and how much we will advance in His service and praise when left without the generous reward of consolations"; and
3. "God wishes to give us a true knowledge and understanding of ourselves." (*Spiritual Exercises* 322)

Desolation means feeling disconsolate and empty.

Leadership Lesson

A leadership lesson to be derived from the Ignatian idea of desolation:

Patience protects the self-aware leader from an unwise reversal of course when darkness sets in; the absence of hope, faith, and love signals the need to wait patiently for clarity and a certain stillness of soul before taking action.

REFLECTION

"Wait for the LORD; / be strong, and let your heart take courage; / wait for the LORD!" (Ps 27:14).

13

Love

Take, Lord, and receive
all my liberty, my memory,
my understanding, and my entire will,
all that I have and possess.
Thou hast given all to me.
To Thee, O Lord, I return it.
All is Thine, dispose of it wholly
according to Thy will.
Give me Thy love and Thy grace,
for this is sufficient for me.

~ Spiritual Exercises 234

St. Ignatius provides a famous pre-note to the "Contemplation to Attain the Love of God": "Before presenting this exercise it will be good to call attention to two points: 1. The first is that love ought to manifest itself in deeds rather than in words. 2. The second is that love consists in a mutual sharing of goods, for example, the lover gives and shares with the beloved what he possesses, or something of that which he has or is able to give; and vice versa, the beloved shares with the lover....Thus one always gives to the other" (*Spiritual Exercises* 230–31).

Ignatius then places the one making the Exercises "in the presence of God our Lord and of His angels and saints" (no. 232). Then he has the retreatant ask "for an intimate knowledge of the many blessings received, that filled with gratitude for all, I may in all things love and serve the Divine Majesty" (no. 233). Next, "I will ponder with great affection how much God our Lord has done for me, and how much He has given me of what He possesses, and finally, how much, as far as He can, the same Lord desires to give Himself to me according to His divine decrees. Then I will reflect upon myself, and consider, according to all reason and justice, what I ought to offer the Divine Majesty, that is, all I possess and myself with it. Thus, as one would do who is moved by great feeling, I will make this offering of myself" (no. 234).

Next, Ignatius directs the retreatant "to reflect how God dwells in creatures: in the elements giving them existence, in the plants giving them life, in the animals conferring upon them sensation, in man bestowing understanding. So He dwells in me and gives me being, life, sensation, intelligence; and makes a temple of me, besides having created me in the likeness and image of the Divine Majesty" (no. 235). This awareness prompts one to pray, in the words quoted above: "Take, Lord, and receive...."

Leadership Lesson

The leadership lessons to be drawn from these considerations:

Leadership is an act of love. Reminders of God's love are everywhere in creation. Leadership, as an exercise of love, is a privileged way to encounter the presence of God in both leader and led.

REFLECTION

"Love is what you've been through with someone." Do you agree?

14

Love Will Decide Everything

*Nothing is more practical than finding God, that is,
than falling in love in a quite absolute, final way.
What you are in love with, what seizes your
    imagination,
will affect everything.
It will decide what will get you out of bed in the
    morning,
what you will do with your evenings,
how you will spend your weekends,
what you will read,
who you know,
what breaks your heart,
and what amazes you with joy and gratitude.
So fall in love, stay in love, and it will decide
    everything.*
~ Pedro Arrupe, Superior General of the
Society of Jesus, 1965–1983

Pedro Arrupe was a great Jesuit leader. Like St. Ignatius, he led from a desk in Rome, although modern means of travel enabled him to visit Jesuit works worldwide. His above reflection is rooted in his own prayerful consideration over the years of the "Contemplation to Attain the Love of God," which was with him at the desk and in all his travels.

Leadership Lesson

From this reflection, several Ignatian leadership lessons flow:

Love sets priorities. Without priorities, leadership energy is dissipated. Pedro Arrupe suggests that if love sets the leadership agenda, it "will decide everything."

REFLECTION

Are you comfortable in the freedom that God's love provides, or do you seek refuge in rule and obedience to authority?

15

Leadership Qualities of a Jesuit General

In the Constitutions of the Society of Jesus, *authored by Ignatius, the qualities to be found in a superior general are listed. Among them are: union with God in prayer; love of fellow Jesuits; humility; self-control; magnanimity and fortitude of soul; understanding and judgment; discretion; being "vigilant and solicitous to undertake enterprises"; being energetic; "reputation, high esteem and whatever else aids toward prestige with those within and without [the Society]"; being "outstanding in every virtue."*

"If any of these aforementioned qualities should be wanting, there should at least be no lack of great probity and of love for the Society, nor of good judgment accompanied by sound learning."

~ see pt. IX, chap. 2, nos. 723–35

After outlining the ideals relating to the one who governs and the style of governance, the *Constitutions* states, "He will achieve this kind of government primarily by the influence and example of his life, by his charity and love of the Society..., by his prayer..., and by his sacrifices" (no. 790). It is also worth noting that Ignatius acknowledged the importance of prestige in support of effective leadership, while insisting that both good reputation and prestige be grounded in humility.

Leadership Lesson

The leadership lessons to be drawn from these criteria:

There is no substitute for good character in a leader. Love of the organization and its members is essential, as are magnanimity of spirit and generosity of heart. Prestige and good reputation are not to be disdained by a leader, just contained within humility.

REFLECTION

There can be no leadership without followership. How does a leader enable others to follow?

16

Choice or "Election"

In the Spiritual Exercises, there is the "Introduction to Making a Choice of a Way of Life" (no. 169), a section on "Matters about Which a Choice Should be Made" (nos. 170–74), another section on "Three Times When a Correct and Good Choice of a Way of Life May be Made" (nos. 175–77), and still another dealing with "Two Ways of Making a Choice of a Way of Life in the Third Time [a time of tranquility]" which includes the "First Way of Making a Good and Correct Choice of a Way of Life (nos. 178–83) and the "Second Way of Making a Correct and Good Choice of a Way of Life" (nos. 184–88).

"There are things that fall under an unchangeable choice, such as the priesthood, marriage, etc. There are others with regard to which our choice may be changed, for example, to accept or relinquish a benefice, to receive or renounce temporal goods" (*Spiritual Exercises* 171). Our leadership concern here is with choices that "may be changed."

The three times when a "correct and good" choice of a way of life may be made are:

1. when God "so moves and attracts the will that a devout soul without hesitation, or the possibility of hesitation, follows what has been manifested to it";
2. when "much light and understanding are derived through experience of desolations

and consolations and discernment of diverse
spirits"; and

3. in a "time of tranquility....A time when the
   soul is not agitated by different spirits, and
   has free and peaceful use of its natural
   powers" (nos. 175–77).

Focusing now on making a "choice subject to
change" and making it in a "time of tranquility," the following guidelines are helpful:

1. "It is necessary to keep as my aim the end for
   which I am created";
2. "I must be indifferent";
3. "I should be like a balance at
   equilibrium...ready to follow whatever I
   perceive is more for the glory and praise of
   God and the salvation of my soul."
4. After weighing the advantages and
   disadvantages, "I will consider which
   alternative appears more reasonable...and
   come to a decision in the matter under
   deliberation because of weightier motives
   presented to my reason, and not
   because of any sensual inclination"
   (nos. 179, 182).

There are four additional rules:

1. "The love that moves...one to choose must
   descend from above, that is, from the love of
   God";
2. "I should represent to myself someone I have
   never seen or known, and whom I would like
   to see practice all perfection" and tell that
   person what is best to do and then do the
   same myself;
3. Next, "consider what...action I would wish to
   have followed in making the present choice if

I were at the moment of death" and make my decision accordingly;

4. Finally, place myself in the "presence of my judge on the last day, and reflect what decision in the present matter I would then wish to have made" (nos. 184–87).

Leadership Lesson

The leadership lesson related to all of this: In a time of tranquility, the will of the leader can become aligned with the will of God. When that happens, good choices will be made.

REFLECTION

Making decisions is the business of leadership.

17

Admonitor

*The Society should have with the superior
general...some person who...[a]fter he has had
recourse to God in prayer...[will] admonish the
general about anything in him which he thinks will
be more conducive to greater service and glory to
God. The general in turn ought to be content with
what is provided.*

~ Constitutions of the Society of Jesus,
pt. IX, chap. 4, no. 770

The above excerpt from the *Constitutions* comes from the
hand of Ignatius and refers to what he called the "provi-
dent care" that the Society should exercise in regard to
the superior general. The caring function is called admonition; the person who exercises this care is called the
admonitor. Note that the admonitor has no authority but
enjoys the confidence of the general. He has access to the
general at any time. And note further that the general
"ought to be content" to have an admonitor.

The motivation for all of this is to assure that the
Society's service to others is the best possible.

Leadership Lesson

The leadership lesson to be derived from the existence of this function is that every leader should have someone who is willing and able to tell him in confidentiality and with absolute freedom the unvarnished truth. The organization suffers in a situation where "even your best friend won't tell you."

REFLECTION

Assuming there is someone nearby who is charged with the responsibility of admonition, to what extent is it the responsibility of the leader to make sure that admonition is offered on a regular basis?

18

Globalization

To be able to meet the spiritual needs of souls in many regions with greater facility and with greater security for those who go among them for this purpose, the superiors of the Society...will have authority to send any of the Society's members whomsoever to whatsoever place these superiors think it more expedient to send them.

~ *Constitutions* 618

To proceed more successfully in this sending of subjects to one place or another, one should keep the greater service of God and the more universal good as the norm to hold before his eyes as the norm to hold oneself on the right course.

~ *Constitutions* 622a

The more universal the good is, the more it is divine. Therefore preference ought to be given to those persons and places which, through their own improvement, become a cause which can spread the good accomplished to many others who are under their influence or take guidance from them.

~ *Constitutions* 622d

The expression, "the more universal the good is, the more it is divine," (*quo univeralius, eo divinius*) is a classic Ignatian principle. Ignatius, in incorporating this phrase into the *Constitutions of the Society of Jesus*, gives further evidence of his global perspective, always seeking broader influence, a wider reach, the greater good, and of course, the greater glory of God. He therefore takes a "whomsoever–whatsoever" approach to apostolic assignments, not in the sense that anyone can do anything anywhere, but in the more magnanimous outlook that no one should be held in one place when there is greater need and greater good to be achieved by this one in some other (often more distant) place.

Leadership Lesson

The leadership lesson to be taken from *quo universalius, eo divinius*:

Not only is the "big picture" important for effective leadership, casting the leadership net as widely as possible is characteristic of Ignatian leadership.

REFLECTION

Travel and reading are ways for a leader to experience the *quo universalius* stretch. What might be good to read, and where might a willing leader be advised to travel?

19

Our Way of Proceeding

Certain attitudes, values, and patterns of behavior join together to become what has been called the Jesuit way of proceeding. The characteristics of our way of proceeding were born in the life of St. Ignatius and shared by his first companions. Jerome Nadal writes that "the form of the Society is in the life of Ignatius." "God set him up as a living example of our way of proceeding."
~ Decree 26, *34th General Congregation of the Society of Jesus* (1995)

The expression "our way of proceeding" was used by Ignatius in the *Constitutions* and elsewhere. The thirty-fourth General Congregation summarized this "way" by employing the following set of headings in its twenty-sixth Decree titled, "Characteristics of our Way of Proceeding":

1. Deep Personal Love for Jesus Christ;
2. Contemplative in Action;
3. An Apostolic Body in the Church;
4. Solidarity with Those Most in Need;
5. Partnership with Others;
6. Called to Learned Ministry;
7. Men Sent, Always Available for New Missions;
8. Ever Searching for the *Magis*.

The "Conclusion" to Decree 26 reads, "Our way of proceeding is a way of challenge." But "this way of proceeding is the reason why every son of the Society will always act and react in a consistently Jesuit and Ignatian way, even in the most unforeseen circumstances."[2]

Leadership Lesson

The leadership lesson to be drawn from "our way of proceeding" is contained in this prayer of Pedro Arrupe:

Lord, meditating on "our way of proceeding,"
I have discovered that the ideal of our way of
acting is your way of acting.
Give me that *sensus Christi* that I may
feel with your feelings,
With the sentiments of your heart, which basically
are love for your Father
And love for all men and women.
Teach me how to be compassionate to the suffering,
to the poor, the blind, the lame, and the lepers.
Teach us your way so that it becomes our way today,
so that we may come closer to the great
ideal of St. Ignatius:
to be companions of Jesus, collaborators
in the work of redemption.

REFLECTION

A secular way of saying this is "you can't steer a parked car." So get yourself in gear and get going!

20

The Manner Is Ordinary

For good reasons, having always in view God's greater service, the manner of living as to external things is ordinary....

~ St. Ignatius of Loyola,
Institute (Rule) *of the Society of Jesus,*
chap. 1, no. 8.

The full text of this rule goes on to specify that there are no regular penances or austerities required of Jesuits, as was typically the case in other religious orders. Fasts and penances could weaken a person and impede apostolic effectiveness. Moreover, it was the personal experience of Ignatius that certain austerities and penitential practices repelled others and hindered the greater good. Jesuits, while living their vow of poverty, were to dress and follow a lifestyle comparable to diocesan priests.

"The manner is ordinary" translates practically into an absence of privilege and perquisites; it mandates the use of material things in a way that makes the Jesuit available as well as accountable to those he is there to serve.[3]

Leadership Lesson

A leadership lesson to be drawn from the Ignatian expression "the manner is ordinary" is that the purpose of leadership is service, and they lead most effectively who refuse to let themselves enjoy a lifestyle that is too far removed in privilege and possessions from those they hope to serve.

REFLECTION

The whole world saw this lesson exemplified in the simple choice made by Pope Francis when he paid his own hotel bill upon checking out at the end of the conclave that elected him pope. Similarly, his scaled-down lifestyle as pope has had an enormously positive impact.

The Third Degree of Humility

The third mode of humility is the most perfect. It consists in this. If we suppose the first and second kind attained, then whenever the praise and glory of God would be equally served, in order to imitate and be in reality more like Christ our Lord, I desire and choose poverty with Christ poor, rather than riches; insults with Christ loaded with them, rather than honors; I desire to be accounted as worthless and a fool for Christ, rather than to be esteemed as wise and prudent in this world. So Christ was treated before me.

~ Spiritual Exercises 167

According to St. Ignatius, there are three levels of alignment of one's will with the will of God. The first is necessary for salvation. "I so subject and humble myself as to obey the law of God our Lord in all things" (*Spiritual Exercises* 165). This level of humility is thus understood as obedience to God's will. The second kind or degree of humility means "that I neither desire nor am I inclined to have riches rather than poverty, to seek honor rather than dishonor, to desire a long life rather than a short life, provided only in either alternative I would promote equally the service of God our Lord and the salvation of my soul" (no. 166). This is what we've seen earlier in this book as "indifference"—humility thus understood eliminates one's own desire as finally decisive. The third or highest degree of humility, outlined above, implies the desire to be like Christ who is poor, despised, and deemed foolish.

This third is a high level or degree of sanctity—a goal to be sought, a condition to be valued. Ignatius says that the one making the Exercises "should beg our Lord to deign to choose him [or her] for this kind of humility... provided equal praise and service be given to the Divine Majesty" (no.168). This is a way of saying simply that Christ is the norm.

Leadership Lesson

The following leadership lesson can be derived from a consideration of the Third Degree of Humility:

In a secular setting completely unrelated to the context of Ignatian spirituality, namely, a back-office service company, SEI Investments, in Oak, Pennsylvania, the word *humbition* is held up for praise and imitation. "At SEI, the most effective leaders exude a blend of humility and ambition—humbition—that relies on the power of persuasion rather than formal authority."[4] The Ignatian leadership principle that is relevant here is that humility, as demonstrated in the life of Christ, is a highly desirable leadership characteristic. Think of it as "humbition."

REFLECTION

Does the notion of "humbition" provide a
practical way of relating the countercultural values
of Ignatian spirituality to workplace life?

Notes

1. Eknath Easwaran, *Gandhi the Man: How One Man Changed Himself to Change the World* (Tomales, CA: Nilgiri Press, 2011), 136.

2. Pedro Arrupe, "Our Way of Proceeding," *AR* 17, no. 55 (1979): 719.

3. This famous phrase was used by Jesuit Father John LaFarge as the title for his 1954 autobiography.

4. See William C. Taylor and Polly LaBarre, *Mavericks at Work* (New York: Harper Paperback, 2008), 240.